THE JEWISH HOLOCAUST
FOR BEGINNERS

WRITERS AND READERS PUBLISHING, INC.
P.O. Box 461, Village Station
New York, NY 10014

Writers and Readers Limited
9 Cynthia Street
London N1 9JF
England

A Writers and Readers Documentary Comic Book Copyright © 1995

ISBN # 0-86316-182-0

0 1 2 3 4 5 6 7 8 9

Manufactured in the United States of America

Beginners Documentary Comic Books are published by Writers and Readers Publishing, Inc. Its trademark, consisting of the words "For Beginners, Writers and Readers Documentary Comic Books" and the Writers and Readers logo, is registered in the U.S. Patent and Trademark Office and in other countries.

THE JEWISH HOLOCAUST
FOR BEGINNERS

BY STUART JUSTMAN
ILLUSTRATED BY REBECCA SHOPE

On February 21, 1944, three months after the Jews of
Italy were officially declared an alien race, some 600 held at the
detention camp in Fossoli were notified that they would be transported the following day. For each person unaccounted for in the
morning roll-call, ten would be shot.

As was their custom, the Germans did not tell the Jews
of Fossoli their destination—the gas chambers of Auschwitz. To
have spoken truthfully would have violated the Germans' habit of
deception and their policy of giving orders not explanations.
Nevertheless a sentence of death hung palpably over the camp.

And so the Jews of Fossoli passed the night readying
themselves for death, each in their own fashion. Some prayed.
It is said, though, that the women of the camp used the night to
wash clothes in preparation for the journey to death, so that
when morning came the barbed wire was hung with the children's laundry.

Germany's defeat in World War I left the country shaken. In the words of William Pfaff, "The uncertainty of Germans about the identity and 'purpose' of Germany" now amounted to a crisis. Long haunted by the question of its mission, Germany soon found one. The mission of Germany became a death mission. With its imperative to kill all the Jews of Europe from one end to the other, from Italy to the Baltic, Nazism laid to rest with a vengeance the long uncertainty of the Germans.

The Holocaust is the term given to the systematic murder of European Jewry, mostly during the years 1942-45, in the name of Germany's racial mission. The event is like no other, beyond precedent or analogy, an abyss in history itself. As unique as the Holocaust is, however, it did not simply spring into existence but followed from a series of measures taken by the Nazis from the time of their rise to power in 1933. The Nazis built up to the Holocaust.

Some object to the word "Holocaust" on the ground that it is originally a biblical term for a burnt offering or sacrifice, a notion grotesque or even impious as applied to the murdered Jews. Considering, though, that the original meaning has been forgotten (as is usual in the evolution of words) and that "Holocaust" has passed into common usage not as a term of derision but as a word for a slaughter terrible beyond all precedent and beyond the power of other words to name—considering all this, I have retained this disputed word.

Two parallel chains of events in Germany of the 1930s lead to the Holocaust: the stripping of Jews' civic status bit by bit and Nazi experiments with methods of controlled killing. The first would ultimately leave Jews so

naked, so bereft of legal status, that the inmates of Auschwitz did not possess the right to a spoon. The second ordained that those shipped to Auschwitz, like the Jews of Fossoli, would lose not just their spoons but their very teeth.

In the 1930s the Nazis took one measure after another nullifying the rights of German Jews and marking them with public hatred. For example:

• In 1933, the year the Nazis came to power, Jews were barred from the civil service and public office.

• In the Nuremberg Laws of 1935 Jews were deprived of citizenship and forbidden to marry or have sexual relations with persons of German blood (as though the Jews were not themselves Germans).

• In 1936 Jews lost the right to vote.

• In 1938 Jews were barred from business, law and medicine. The expulsion of Jews from medicine was especially fateful since it left the field to the types who were to preside over the mass murder of the Jews, justify it as a health measure, and give Auschwitz its cover as a medical center.

The New York News

NEW YORK, FRIDAY, NOVEMBER 11, 1938

NAZIS LOOT, BURN JEWISH SHOPS, HOMES, TEMPLES

All Vienna's Synagogues Attacked; Jews are Beaten, Homes and Shops are Destroyed, Looted

On November 9, 1938 was the infamous Kristallnacht, or Night of Broken Glass, in which some 20,000 Jews across Germany were arrested, "Jewish windows" were smashed and synagogues burned at the behest of Hitler's propaganda minister, Goebbels. Fire crews stood by at the synagogues to keep the flames from spreading to non-Jewish property. So obsessive was the assault on the rights of the Jews that in 1938 their driver's licenses were revoked, by 1939 they were banned from public parks and libraries, and by 1941 forbidden to use the telephone; so thorough was the effort to eradicate all traces of the Jews that it is said that in all of Berlin only two signs with the word "Jewish" remained by 1945.

• The process of marking Jews as aliens was completed in 1941 with the decree requiring them to wear a yellow badge. (In their mania for marking, the Nazis also gave all male Jews the middle name of Israel and all female Jews that of Sarah.) At this point they were literally marked for death, for the technology of killing was nearing completion.

Some refugees from Hitler:

Freud. Einstein.
Thomas Mann. Bertolt Brecht.
Hannah Arendt. Erich Fromm.
Hans Bethe, later recipient of the
Nobel Prize in theoretical physics.
Herbert Marcuse, guru of the student
revolt of the 1960s.

Just as the Jews were stripped, by a fatal progression, of legal status, property, life, and finally even graves (for their bodies were dug up and burned), so Nazi methods of killing unfolded in a demonic progression that ended with the gas chamber. In fact the Nazis began with a kind of pre-killing, sterilization.

•Within six months of Hitler's coming to power, a law was passed ordering the sterilization (that is, the extermination over time) of those deemed physically or mentally defective.

•The next phase was the killing of children with physical or mental disabilities. Under this program some thousands of children were "granted a mercy death," generally by sedating drugs.

•Next, under the T4 program, the killing was extended to adult patients deemed "unworthy of life." By now the preferred means of execution was gassing. At the same time all Jewish patients whatever in German institutions were ruled subject to death, under the pretense that the killing of undesirables was a medical imperative, a measure required for the health of the German body politic.

Germans pass by the broken shop window of a Jewish-owned business that was destroyed during Kristallnacht.

Memo from Hitler, Sept. 1, 1939

"Reichsleiter Bouhler and Dr. Brandt, MD, are charged with the responsibility of enlarging the authority of certain physicians to be designated by name in such a manner that persons who, according to human judgment, are incurable, can, upon a most careful diagnosis of their condition of sickness, be accorded a mercy death."

Jewish women and their children from Mizocz, undressed in preparation for their execution

In an interview in 1971, one of the T4 bureaucrats, Franz Stangl—later commandant of Treblinka—reverted to the same phrasing. His superior explained to him (Stangl said) "that the only patients affected were those who after the most careful examination—a series of four tests carried out by at least two physicians—were considered absolutely incurable so that, he assured me, a totally painless death represented a real release." The most careful examination turned out to be a charade. The photographic resemblance between between Stangl's language and that of a memo of decades before points to the formulaic nature of Nazi code and its power to imprint itself on the mind.

• In 1941 the T4 program itself was extended to concentration camps under the code name of 14f13. At this point, with much of Europe already under Nazi occupation, the technology for the mass murder of the Jews (gassing), the rationale (medical necessity), and the procedure (bureaucratic routine more lawful than law itself) were all in place. Only the death factories were needed to carry them out to their conclusion. As one measure led to another, events developed such a criminal "logic" that many a German involved in these preliminaries for Auschwitz must have tried to convince himself in later years that he had been swept along in the racing current of history—a more fitting description of what befell the Jews.

"I certainly suspected nothing like what happened later on," said Adolf Eichmann, all virginal innocence, looking back on his actions in 1940.

Is it possible to end the life of a people as if by sterilization, but without having to wait for them to die out in their own time? Can murder itself be made a sanitary procedure? While the Nazis worked on these questions (whose answer was the gas chamber) through the 1930s and into the next decade, they were also testing how far they themselves were willing to go, how well their system of pretexts and deceptions worked, and how much they could get away with. The results of their inquiries emboldened them to proceed to the very end.

With the Jews stripped of human status and with the discovery of the terrible efficacy of gas, the Nazis were poised for what they called "the Final Solution of the Jewish Problem." It was at the Wannsee Conference, held in Berlin on January 20, 1942, that a plan for the complete annihilation of the Jews of Europe was adopted. Minutes of the conference read in part:

In the course of the final solution, the Jews should be brought under appropriate direction in a suitable manner to the east [that is, Poland] for labor utilization. Separated by sex, the Jews capable of work will be led into these areas in large labor columns to build roads, whereby doubtless a large part will fall away through natural reduction.

The inevitable final remainder which doubt-less constitutes the toughest element will have to be dealt with appropriately.

As though the annihilation of the Jews were a cause too holy to be spoken of by name, the Nazis used code-words like these to refer to it. By such directives was the fate of European Jewry decided. By 1945 when the Nazis were defeated, they had killed ten thousand times the six hundred Jews of Fossoli who perished that February in Auschwitz.

Arriving transport of Jews at the death camp in Chelmno, Poland, 1940.

Years later Adolf Eichmann, the convener of the Wannsee Conference, was interrogated about the meaning of the sentences just quoted.

Q: What is meant by "natural reduction"?

A: That's perfectly normal dying. Of a heart attack or pneumonia, for instance. If I were to drop dead just now, that would be natural reduction.

Q: If a man is forced to perform heavy physical labor and not given enough to eat—he grows weaker, he gets so weak that he has a heart attack—

A: That would undoubtedly have been reported as natural reduction.

Q: What does "dealt with appropriately" mean?

A: That . . . that . . . that comes from Himmler. Natural selection— that's . . . that was his hobby.

Q: Yes, but what does it mean here?

A: Killed, killed, undoubtedly.

In addition to the Jews, the Nazis murdered prisoners of war, innumerable Russian civilians, political prisoners, common criminals, Jehovah's Witnesses, homosexuals, vagrants, and some 100,000 Gypsies, among others. No one knows how many in all perished at the hands of the Nazis, but whatever it is, the total greatly exceeded the roughly six

million Jews. But six million is in itself a prodigious figure. Because of the Nazis' systematic effort to eradicate the Jews from the earth—an undertaking like no other in human history—it is the Jews who are the focus of this study. When the Nazis first unleashed their killers, they went straight for the Jews.

By the Nazis' own calculations, the Jewish population of Europe was concentrated most heavily in "the East"—Poland and the Soviet Union. Accordingly it was in the sectors of the Soviet Union occupied by the Germans following the invasion in June 1941 that the mass killing of Jews began in earnest. These executions were not, however, carried out in factory-complexes like Auschwitz but by mobile killing squads, the so-called Einsatzgruppen. Documentary evidence shows that a single squad, Einsatzgruppe 3, murdered at least 138,272 people beginning in July 1941. No one, again, can say how many were slain by the Einstazgruppen, but the total was certainly many times that figure. To chronicle such crimes exceeds the capacity of human speech. The tongue withers.

Let one incident, therefore, serve for many.
        Upon reaching the small town of Koritz on July 2, 1941, the Germans proceeded swiftly against the Jews, then numbering some five thousand.

After one of the ensuing massacres, the Germans notified the Jewish council of Koritz that the dead had not been properly buried: the pits needed more earth. And so, writes one of the witnesses,

We all mobilized for this sacred task. What we saw there, so I believe, has no parallel in the annals of the extermination of European Jewry. Three pits were revealed to us: in one men were buried; in the second, women; and in the third, children. They had propped up the old man [Rabbi] Shiher on the mass grave of the men. He sat there upright and the wind moved his white beard to and fro. At first sight he seemed to be alive, praying, lamenting, shrieking, crying out and condemning Heaven for the terrible slaughter.

But the Rabbi of Koritz was dead. He moved as if with the rocking motion of prayer because men buried beneath him were still alive. "The pits heaved and sank, heaved and sank. These were the last convulsions of the dying."

To set up this effigy of a Rabbi in prayer; to deride the dead and the not-yet dead; to make Jews witnesses and instruments of their own humiliation— these were Nazi flourishes.

At one time the Nazis entertained thoughts of "solving the Jewish problem" by pressuring Jews to emigrate or even transplanting them en masse to

Madagascar. With the commencement of war, as millions
of Jews in Eastern Europe fell into Nazi hands, German
policy called for concentrating the captives in ghettoes.
Subjected there to hunger, hard labor, and disease, they
were expected to die off by what the Nazis called natural
reduction. Soon enough, however, the Germans set in
motion a method to produce the deaths of those who failed
to succumb "naturally."

The mass of the killings carried out by the Nazis took place, as we know, not by the sides of roads but in sealed chambers. Killing was transformed into an industrial process, with all of the repetition and all of the concentration on the end product that characterize factory production. The end product in this case was ashes. Auschwitz represents the industrialization of death.

Inmates at forced labor in the Mauthausen concentration camp, Mauthausen, Austria, summer 1942.

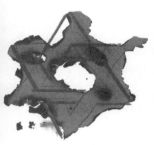

Why did the Nazis turn from the machine-gun to the gas canister? Why did they go to the trouble of constructing killing centers like Auschwitz and transporting Jews there from all directions? Perhaps they took pleasure in reversing the Jewish story of exodus—the journey away from enslavement and forced labor. In any case "processing" the Jews of Europe through the death factories satisfied the Germans' love of method. And the alternative of hunting the Jews down and killing them wherever they lived may have been politically distasteful, for murdering millions in plain day in the middle of Europe (rather than "the East") would have blown the entire system of denials and concealments, code-words and state secrets in which the Nazis covered what they did.

Additionally, though, the gas chamber offered a "clean" mode of killing—a medically supervised death that not only accorded well with the sanitary pretensions of the killers but left no blood on their hands. There are reports of members of the Einsatzgruppen traumatized by their own acts. The executioners themselves sickened.

In an effort to clean up the record, the Nazis had prisoners open the mass graves of their victims and burn the bodies, after which the prisoners themselves were put to death. In Sobibor, before the Nazis had their methods down to a science, crews of prisoners were made to bury corpses in lime-pits, and then were murdered themselves. The crematorium economized these procedures.

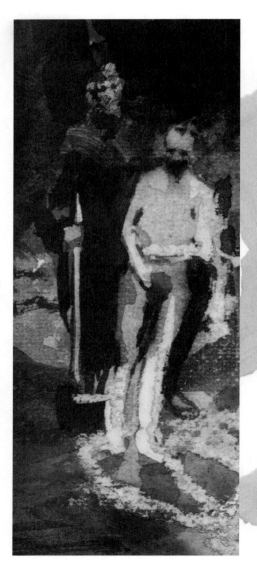

Rudolf Höss, the commandant of Auschwitz, later said, "I was relieved to think that we were to be spared all these blood baths, and that the victims too would be spared suffering until the last moments came." But one doubts somehow that gassing was intended as a kindness toward the Jews.

Operation of the extermination camps began in 1942.

(Concentration camps, on the other hand, had been in existence since 1933, Dachau being the first.)

The popular image of the death camp is an accurate one: barracks to house the as-yet living; prison yard; electrified fences topped with barbed wire; SS patrols, with dogs; watch towers; search lights; the entire compound served by rail lines and presided over by the chimneys of the crematoria as if by infernal steeples.

In industrial terms, rail cars supplied the raw material and the finished product went up the chimney as ash.

In the barracks were kept all those not killed immediately upon arrival but who almost certainly would be killed sooner or later if they did not succumb to "natural reduction" by starvation and disease. This includes slave laborers. The Nazis did not commute their death sentence, only postponed its execution for a time. For in the final analysis the Jews were not at Auschwitz to render economic value but to swell the number of the dead. The few who survived did so by chance as much as anything else. Among the inmates of Auschwitz there was a grim joke: **"There is no escape but through the chimney."**

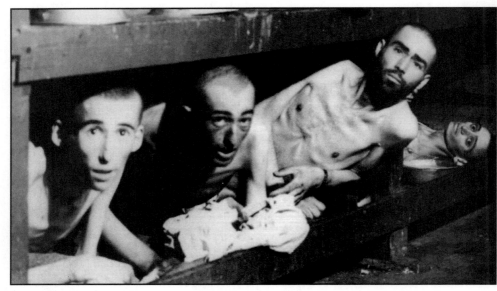
Survivors being liberated at the Buchenwald camp, April 16, 1945

A survivor of Dachau and Buchenwald, Bruno Bettelheim, came to the conclusion that for those who ran the concentration camps terror was "only a means for attaining certain ends," such as to strike fear into the population at large. In the extermination camps, however, death became virtually an end in itself: the chimney was their true reason for being. This fatal progression from the use of terror as a political expedient to wholesale slaughter is entirely characteristic of Nazism.

As the Nazis put the Jews under arrest country by country, they made use of the Jewish Councils (Judenräte), the governing bodies of the local Jewish communities. Compelled to "co-operate," the Councils handed over Jews as well as treasure to the Nazis.

Why, apart from the motive of extortion, did the captors act out this charade of co-operation, this cynical pretense of respect for the collective autonomy of the Jews? Perhaps for tactical reasons. By turning Jew against Jew (as they also did systematically in the camps themselves), the Nazis played divide and conquer. Things went smoother, too, when the Councils "facilitated" the Nazis' scheme. By flattering the Councils' false hopes that they could somehow negotiate with the Nazis or ransom Jewish lives, the Nazis expedited the process of deportation while incidentally having a sadistic laugh at the Jews' expense. And this points to a deeper reason.

For the Nazis it was not enough that the Jews should be killed, but they must also be stripped of dignity—violated. In the case of the co-opting of the Councils, this meant that the leaders of the Jews must be made puppets like the Rabbi of Koritz, must come and go at the behest of their captors, and especially must be made to betray their trust and hand over the lives of the Jews in their care. Like Winston Smith in the torture cell in Orwell's 1984, the leaders of the Jews must be forced to say in effect, "Kill someone else and not me!" When he utters these words of betrayal, Winston Smith is broken forever, and it is possible that the Nazis intended the same effect for the venerated leaders of the

Jews. Killing the Jews was not enough: they must also be complicit in the execution of their own brethren.

The extremes of complicity were reached, however, within Auschwitz itself, where "Special Squads" of prisoners (in Nazi jargon "Sonderkommandos") were responsible for the dirty work of death—everything from pulling gold teeth from the dead to removing ashes from the ovens. Some entrusted with these duties must have felt defiled beyond any possibility of cleansing or expiation.

Some may have considered themselves favored by the SS, exempted from the death meted out to everyone else. Their exemption was but temporary.

In due course the squads were themselves murdered, to be succeeded by another. Far from being privileged as they may have imagined, the assistants of the SS were being set up—given a good long look at the abyss before being thrust in themselves.

On the basis of his own observations, it was Bettelheim's judgment that the concentration camps were "laboratories" for breaking people and producing complicity. He tells, for example, of long-term prisoners who tried to make SS costumes for themselves out of scraps of their guards' uniforms: a graphic image of complicity with the captor. Some prisoners, too, had a vested interest in the murder of their comrades, like a young craftsman in Sobibor who was kept alive to work the gold taken from the dead.

This prisoner of Dachau was subjected to low pressure experimentation where air pressures were created comprarable to those at 15,000 meters in altitude. These experiments were conducted to determine how high airplane pilots could survive without oxygen.

Dachau, Germany, 1942.

Jews were shipped to their death in sealed freight cars, without water, packed so tight that some died standing up and remained standing. Upon their arrival at Auschwitz and their release from the trains (if the word release applies here), the living were filed past one of the SS, often a medical doctor, on the railway platform itself. With a flick of a finger—as slight a motion as pushing a button or checking a box—he sent them either to the right or the left, either to life or death. The name for this fateful ritual was Selection, possibly a

play on Darwin's "natural selection" since only those deemed fit to work were kept alive. The unlucky were soon in the hands of the Special Squads.

A witness tells of the Selection ritual at Auschwitz. One of only a tenth of a transport of Jews to survive the initial sorting, he looked about on the evening of his arrival for his companion. A veteran inmate asked him,

"Was he sent to the left side?"
"Yes," I replied.
"Then you can see him there," I was told.
"Where?"
A hand pointed to the chimney a few hundred yards off, which was sending a column of flame up into the grey sky of Poland.

Nor were those who survived the first Selection saved. They were only reprieved, for soon enough they had to undergo the same ritual over again. As a rule the inmates of Auschwitz could no more evade death than the occupants of a sealed freight car could alter their destination.

And what of the Jews of Fossoli? Within ten minutes of arrival, the men deemed fit had been culled from the group. So far as is known, virtually all the others were swiftly put to death, including even the children whose washing had been done the night before their exodus.

Like the concentration camps before them, the death camps were run by the secret police (the Gestapo), meaning that they were outside the law. The death's-head units of the Guard Corps (the SS), so named after their official insignia, patrolled the camps. To this elite, the most devoted of  Hitler's followers (and breeding stock for the ennoblement of future generations), was entrusted the task of mass murder.

Like an industrial process, the operation of the death camps was reduced to routine. Relentless repetition, for example  constant Selections, served all at once to assure efficiency, to break prisoners psychologically, and to deaden the executioners to the horror of their own actions.

The diary of an SS physician at Auschwitz—one of those who made mass murder seem a public health measure, like controlling tuberculosis—suggests just how routine operations became. It reads in part:

SEPT. 6: Today, an excellent Sunday dinner; tomato soup, one half of chicken with potatoes and red cabbage, and magnificent vanilla ice cream... In the evening at 8:00 attended another special action outdoors.

Even to himself he speaks in code. The "special action" was a Selection in which over 900 French Jews were sent to death, a routine occurrence at Auschwitz. To our diarist the event is less noteworthy than red cabbage.

Franz Stangl, commandant of Treblinka, looking back in 1971: "A transport was normally dealt with in two or three hours. At 12 I had lunch—yes, we usually had meat, potatoes, some fresh vegetables such as cauli-flowers—we grew them ourselves quite soon—and after lunch I had about half an hour's rest." A "transport" contained from 5000 to 6000 people. By "dealt with" Stangl means murdered.

If routines proceed without debate, the severe restriction of discus-sion among the SS themselves cemented the routines of death. As another SS physician at Auschwitz, looking back on his work years later, remarked, only purely technical questions like how best to dispose of corpses were open to discussion.

One had to
burn . . . great piles—enormous piles. Now
that is a great problem, igniting piles of corpses. You can imagine—naked—nothing burns. How does one manage this? ...The
problem was not the selections but how one can burn the colossal quantities if the ovens are not working. That's what was being
talked about, and nothing else.

As he tells of the solution of this problem, we sense the pride of "colossal" achievement rising in him even now, as well as gratitude for the speech-rule that concentrated discussion on purely technical issues the way a tool concentrates force on a point. Like those who were grateful to the Nazis for abolishing freedom—like the German grocer who said, "Before this we had t worry about elections, and parties, and voting. Now we're free"—this SS man seems thankful for the absolute prohibition on moral questioning that made it possible for him and his colleagues to achieve such historical break-

throughs in the incineration of corpses. The "Final Solution" to the problem of the Jews seems to have dictated that not even their bodies should remain, and routines to carry out this supreme imperative were devised by the SS. In principle the elimination of the very corpses of the Jews was to be as ordinary a part of the functioning of Auschwitz as the discharge of waste from a factory. The same SS doctor just quoted went on to say: "The problem of the crematorium and its capacity, etc.—that was equal to the ordinary problem of sewerage and the like elsewhere."

Seed Corn

The Chief of the Gestapo, Heinrich Himmler, notifies his men in 1936, "The existence of sound marriage is futile if it does not result in the creation of numerous descendants. I expect that here, too, the SS and especially the SS leader corps, will serve as guiding example.

"The minimum amount of children for a good sound marriage is four. Should unfortunate circumstances deny a married couple their own children, then every SS leader should adopt racially and hereditarily valuable children and educate them in the spirit of national socialism." Himmler goes on to exhort unmarried women "of good blood" to couple with childless SS men going to the front.

The SS were "selected" to breed as the Jews were "selected" to die.

Among the Italian Jews held at Fossoli and then transported to Auschwitz was Primo Levi, later a great chronicler of the Holocaust. In his book Survival at Auschwitz he writes as one of the damned—one of those the SS considered a disposal problem.

Upon his arrival at Auschwitz Levi is selected to work, stripped of his belongings (even his hair), tattooed and sent for some reason to wait in a hut. Suffering from thirst, he notices a splendid icicle just outside and opens a window to reach for it. At that moment the hand of an SS guard tears the icicle away like contraband. "Why?" asks Levi. What is wrong with sipping on an icicle? The guard, accustomed to giving orders not explanations, retorts, "Hier ist kein warum"—

Here there is no why.

The implied warning seems to be, I could kill you if I chose for opening a window or for any reason at all. I do not have to give reasons. The SS is outside the law.

"Hier ist kein warum."

If the executioners were not to discuss the why of mass murder but simply carry it out with the utmost efficiency, the damned were to submit to the fate prepared for them without asking impertinent questions. Like some god, the sacred cause of mass murder was not to be interrogated.

In warning Primo Levi that Here there is no why, the SS guard revealed a certain twisted truth. For the Jews of Auschwitz there really was no point asking why they were there. They were not transported to Auschwitz for anything they did (though Levi himself had been a partisan, or guerilla), nor even for their religious beliefs, which after all varied from traditional piety to modernism. They were sent to death not because of what they did or what they believed but because of who they were. They were killed for the fact of their birth.

Some numbers that suggest the incomprehensible magnitude of the Holocaust:

- At Auschwitz during July 1944, **12,000** Jews were killed daily.

- Between April 1942 and April 1944 some **1,765,000** Jews were gassed at Auschwitz. (Both of these statistics are findings of the Nuremberg Tribunal following the war.)

- In a December 16, 1941 diary entry, Hans Frank, Governor General of Occupied Poland, estimates the Jews of that region at **3,500,000**. In an January 25, 1944 entry he estimates the Jewish population of occupied Poland at **100,000**.

- In less than two months in 1944, **434,351** Hungarian Jews were transported to Auschwitz in sealed freight cars.

- In the first year of the operation of the first death camp, Chelmno, **145,000** Jews were killed. A quarter million were gassed at Sobibor. The number of known survivors of Chelmno, Belsec, Sobibor, and Treblinka is **87**.

- **30,000** Jews were massacred in Kiev in two days in September 1941—the Babi Yar slaughter.

- Found in but a few of the warehouses of Auschwitz by Allied troops in 1945 were **349,820** men's suits.

- Some **100,000** mental patients, and possibly far more, were put to death in the early phase of the "Final Solution."

When the former SS doctor, interviewed years after the war, remarked that the Jews were considered a problem like sewage, he was no coining a racial insult on the spot but reverting to a formerly official and

deeply established way of thinking and speaking about Jews. In the infamous propaganda film "Jud Süss" Jews are identified with rats, creatures of gutters and sewers.

Even before the Nazis' rise to power there were those who spoke of Jews as toxins, carriers of disease—the old theme of the anti-race, now introduced into an age of mass politics and endowed with an air of "science." When Hitler himself played heavily on bacterial imagery in Mein Kampf, he was not trying out some new figure of speech but working material already in existence, just as a demagogue (which he was) works the fear and rage of his audience. With the argument that the Jews threatened the very life of the German people like a lethal contagion,

Hitler gave his readers the supreme justification for "cleansing" Europe of the Jews—self-defense. Germany must kill the Jews before the Jews kill Germany,

or in other words it must execute upon the Jews the very fate the Jews are secretly devising for the master race. Germany must throw the Jews' plans back at them the way the SS guard was to throw Primo Levi's words back at him: **"Why?" "There is no why."**

And so, in accusing the Jews of "planning the enslavement and with it the destruction of all non-Jewish peoples," Hitler fabricates the justification for doing just that to the Jews. "Only when the international poisoners are exterminated"—international because the Jews form a state unto themselves wherever they reside—will Germany triumph.

In this image of the Jews as an alien body or poison in the body politic we encounter one of the fateful themes of Nazi discourse. The Jew, says Hitler over and over, is "like a noxious bacillus." The "extermination of this pestilence" should already have been carried out. The Jews "poison men's souls like germ-carriers of the worse sort."

Karl Marx, the quintessential Jew, "recognized in the morass of a slowly decomposing world the most essential poisons, extracted them" and prepared a potion for the destruction of healthy races. (In the Nazi imagination the Jews somehow represented both

37

Bolshevism and the stock exchange—a transcendent evil that gave Germany its also-transcendent mission.) From this talk of Jews as deadly germs it is but a step, if that, to Auschwitz, where mass murderers drove cars marked with the Red Cross and the entire operation was camouflaged as a process of disinfection, complete with "showers."

"All great cultures of the past perished only because the originally creative race died out from blood poisoning"

—from Hitler's *Mein Kampf*, a death warrant for European Jewry.

Mein Kampf presents, then, an uncannily explicit and literal premonition of the Holocaust. It is as if this work, though bombastic and unreadable, became the holy writ of Nazism, its every word possessing the imperative force of an utterance "divinely inspired." Even the early stages of the Holocaust, the sterilization and "euthanasia" programs, are directly prefigured in Mein Kampf. "The demand that defective people be prevented from propagating equally defective offspring is a demand of the clearest reason and if systematically executed represents the most humane act of mankind." Hence the sterilization program. (Notice here the pretense of mercy, albeit not to the "defectives" themselves.) The systematic killing of the sick, as in the T4 program, is authorized in the same paragraph. "If necessary," writes Hitler, "the incurably sick will be pitilessly segregated," by which he surely means something more drastic than mere isolation.

The sterilization of undesirables in the name of racial health; "pitiless" action against the sick; finally the complete extermination of the anti-race—the fatal logic of the Holocaust appears in full in Mein Kampf.

How are we to account for the direct correspondence between Hitler's language and the apocalypse that later struck? Should Hitler be credited with prophetic powers, with mystical insight into those "laws of history" the Nazis claimed to carry out? No. The man's ravings prefigure the Holocaust simply because they became in time the official discourse of power, the coin of the realm.

Все жиды города Ки...
.. его окрестностей долж...
...ы явиться в понедельн...
29 сентября 1941 года к ...
часам утра на угол Мел...
никовой и Доктеривско...
улиц (возле кладбищ).

Взять с собой докуме...
ты, деньги и ценные ве...
.. также теплую одежду...
бельё и пр.

Кто из жидов не выпо...
нит этого распоряжения ..
будет найден в другом мес-
те, будет расстрелян.

Кто из граждан проник-
нет в оставленные жидами
квартиры и присвоит себе
вещи, будет расстрелян.

A sign posted in Kiev instructed the Jews to assemble: "On September 29, 1941, all Jews of the city of Kiev and its outskirts must appear by 8 am at the corner of Melnikov Street and Docterivsky Street . Take along your documents, currency, and valuables, as well as warm clothing, underwear, etc. Any Jew who fails to appear as ordered and is found elsewhere will be shot dead. Anybody who gets into the dwellings abandoned by the Jews and takes belongings there will be shot dead."

Once the Nazis held power Hitler's program was carried out the way an execution follows a death sentence. The "logic" of exterminating a people branded as carriers of disease—a people, moreover, who were alleged to be plotting the death of Germany—must have seemed completely self-evident to those under the sway of Nazi ideology. If endangered by a plague you take sanitary measures. If attacked you defend yourself. Nazi ideology made the Holocaust, a crime of infinite magnitude and inexpressible savagery, seem a mere deduction of the most elementary simplicity.

In her reflections on totalitarianism political philosopher Hannah Arendt (herself a German expatriate) remarks on the comfort to be had in trading the uncertainty of the real world and the freedom of thought for the security of ideology with its "compelling logic." With Germany's defeat in the First World War (attributed by Hitler to the Jews) and the sense of lost foundations that pervaded the next decade, the iron certainties of Hitler's "logic" must indeed have appealed to many.

In Hitler's notorious declaration of intent in a speech of January 30, 1939—"This war will not end as the Jews imagine, namely in the liquidation of all the European and Aryan peoples; the outcome of this war will be the extermination of Jewry"—the rantings of an obscure fanatic are raised to the level of imperial policy.

The image of the Jew as bacteria, used with effect in Mein Kampf, became a constant of Nazi propaganda. Jews were pictured as an alien organism in the body politic, **an internal enemy responsible** (it was said) **for Germany's defeat in the World War.**

So it was that Himmler, chief of the secret police, told high-ranking members of the SS in 1943 that if not for the extermination of the Jews, "we would now probably have reached the 1916-17 stage when the Jews were still in the national body." The Jew is both traitor and plague—more evocative epithets could not have been found—so that the killing of Jews became at once an act of retribution and a health measure like a quarantine.

Jews, captured during the Warsaw ghetto uprising, are led by German soldiers to the assembly point for departaion, April 1943

In ghettoes like Warsaw Jews were in fact quarantined in the sense of being walled in; propaganda campaigns at the time underlined the connection between Jews and typhus. And so when Nazi experimenters injected Jews with typhus in the camps, they could tell themselves it was only just and proper because the Jews had infected the body politic—such was the closed "logic" of the Nazi system of belief. According to the minutes of the Wannsee Conference, "the Jew constitutes a substantial danger as carrier of epidemics."

The British poet T. S. Eliot, once wrote, "The rats are underneath the piles. / The jew is underneath the lot."

Nazi ideology, then, positively dictated the killing of Jews as a matter of public health. As Hannah Arendt has said, in Nazi Germany the commandment became, Thou shalt kill. So literally executed was the commandment to kill Jews as "carriers of epidemics" that the killing agent used in the gas chambers of Auschwitz, a cyanide compound called Zyklon-B, was widely employed to control rodents (the spreaders of the bubonic plague in medieval Europe) and disease-carry-

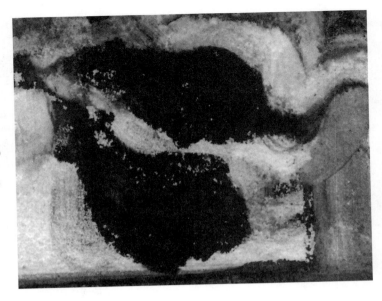

ing insects. The Jews were "exterminated" as you would exterminate pests; or in other words, an elaborate charade of disinfection was enacted by the Nazis. Zyklon-B was distributed, in fact, by the German Corporation for Combating Vermin (its acronym in German, DEGESCH). All of the imagery, both before and after Mein Kampf, casting Jews as spreaders of contagion and biological criminals—all of the identifications of Jews both with vermin and with disease carried by vermin—was brought to realization in the Holocaust.

A present-day expression of the mania for "disinfecting" society by killing undesirables—the so-called ethnic cleansing of Bosnia.

As with the guard's "Here there is no why," a bitter irony underlies the Nazi pretense of curing the body politic by ridding it of the Jews. Such a purification takes place only to the degree

that the community transfers its own crimes onto the Jews—uses them as scapegoats. But this means, of course, that the evils imputed to the Jews, such as their bestiality and thirst for world domination, belong in fact to the Nazis themselves.

So it is that in describing the Jews, the Nazis were apt to paint their own portraits. A striking example is Himmler's account of the soul of the "subhuman" as containing "a brute chaos of wild, unbridled lusts, an inchoate desire to destroy, the most primitive craving, shameless vulgarity." A fair thumbnail sketch of Himmler's master, Hitler himself.

Far from inventing anti-semitism, the Nazis capitalized on a tradition of great historical depth. When they portrayed Jews as a plague, for example, they consciously or unconsciously evoked the medieval libel that the Jews spread the bubonic plague through Europe by secretly poisoning wells. Epithets like "poisoners of the people" in Mein Kampf call up an obscure memory a series of epidemics that took the lives of a frightening proportion of the population of Europe.

One measure of the persistence of anti-semitism is the historical duration of another libel, this one predating even the fourteenth century. According to this legend, the Jews ritually steal Christian children and murder them for their blood.

The story seems to have originated in the twelfth century and taken impetus from the waves of fear aroused by the plagues of the fourteenth. In one version or another the story of ritual murder circulated through d underworld of the European imagination for hundreds of years, even into our own century, flourishing especially in Central Europe.

"Out of this tradition, which particularly in Austria had never died," writes G. R. Elton, **"came Hitler and his brand of anti-semitism."**

In the January 19, 1989 issue of The New York Review of Books, which carries Elton's article, there is an old woodcut of a Jew being hanged upside-down. In Treblinka Jews were hanged upside-down.

In fact the story of the ritual murder was revived for use in Nazi propaganda. In the April 1937 issue of the violently anti-semitic newspaper *Der Stürmer* it appeared in garish detail:

The numerous confessions made by the Jews show that the execution of ritual murders is a law to the Talmud Jew. . . The ritual murders take place especially on the Jewish [holiday of] Purim in memory of the Persian murders, and Passover in memory of the murder of Christ. The instructions are as follows:

The blood of the victims is to be tapped by force. On Passover it is to be used in wine and matzohs. . . [At the table] the head of the family then says, 'Thus we ask God to send the ten plagues to all enemies of the Jewish faith.' Then they eat, and at the end the head of the family exclaims, 'May all Gentiles perish, as the child whose blood is contained in the bread and wine.' . . . Ritual murder is recognized by all Talmud Jews. The Jew believes he absolves himself thus of his sins.

Here again the Nazi portrays himself in his victim: through the slaughter of a scapegoat "he believes he absolves himself of his sins." Note the references to plague, a fear historically associated with the story of ritual murder. Another issue of the same newspaper taught children:

From a Jew's countenance—the evil
   devil talks to us,
The devil, who in every land—is known
   as evil plague.
If we shall be free of the Jew—and
   again will be happy and glad,
Then the youth must struggle—to sub
   due the Jew devil.

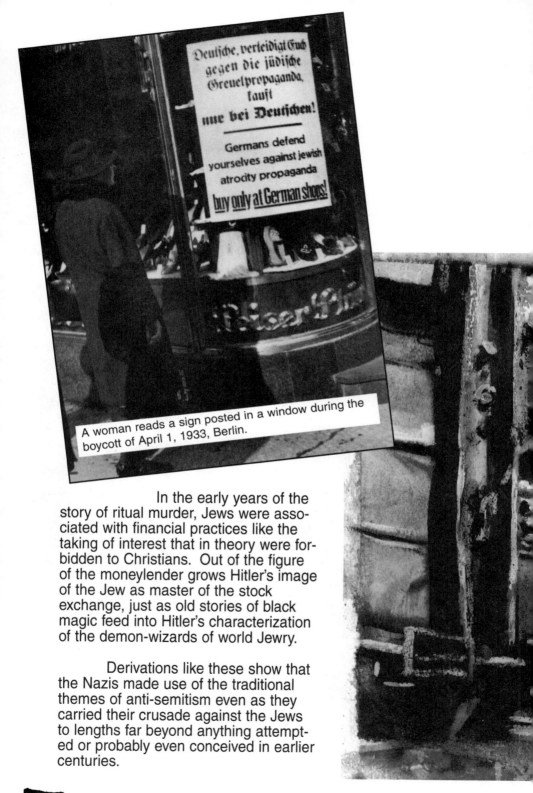

A woman reads a sign posted in a window during the boycott of April 1, 1933, Berlin.

Deutsche, verteidigt Euch
gegen die jüdische
Greuelpropaganda,
kauft
nur bei Deutschen!

Germans defend
yourselves against jewish
atrocity propaganda

buy only at German shops!

In the early years of the story of ritual murder, Jews were associated with financial practices like the taking of interest that in theory were forbidden to Christians. Out of the figure of the moneylender grows Hitler's image of the Jew as master of the stock exchange, just as old stories of black magic feed into Hitler's characterization of the demon-wizards of world Jewry.

Derivations like these show that the Nazis made use of the traditional themes of anti-semitism even as they carried their crusade against the Jews to lengths far beyond anything attempted or probably even conceived in earlier centuries.

The story of ritual murder was originally used to justify killing Jews, and without doubt many died on account of it, but it remained for the Nazis, with their industrial methods, to undertake to annihilate European Jewry as a whole. Similarly, while the Jews had been expelled before—they were banished from England, for example, in 1290 and from Spain in 1492—never had they been subjected to the Nazis' kind of "coordination" and never had they been sent to factories of death. The Holocaust could not have taken place without centuries of bigotry behind it, but it cannot be reduced to events that preceded it and in fact was so unprecedented that the world at large could scarcely believe what unfolded more or less in front of its eyes from 1942 to 1945.

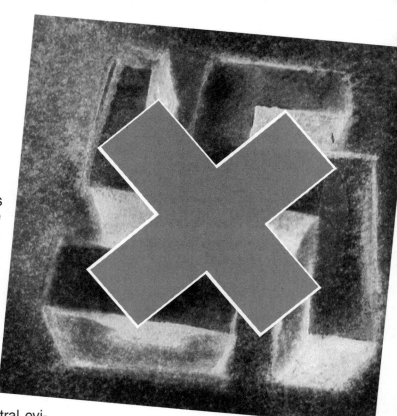

Legend has it that the world was unaware of the Holocaust until the liberators of the camps in 1945 came upon the starved bodies of the living and the spectral evidence of the dead. But this simply does not stand to reason. Although as we well know the Nazis camouflaged the killing operation under code-words and red crosses, the disguise was thin, and in any case millions do not simply vanish from the earth, their eviction from their homes unwitnessed and their murder unreported. It may be that the Nazis incinerated the bodies of the Jews not only to make the "Final Solution" final by removing the last traces of the Jews from the earth, but also to destroy the evidence of their own crimes. Yet the ash was evidence still.

What else but death in any case could have accounted for the millions who were deported to the camps in the full light of day (very often with their property seized by their neighbors) never to be seen again?

In Argentina of the late 1970s and 1980s the thousands kidnapped and murdered by the secret police came to be called "los desaparecidos"—"the disappeared." Yet everyone knew they hadn't just vanished. Unless perhaps a plane goes down in the Pacific, people do not vanish.

This isn't to deny that the Allied troops who came upon the camps in 1945 were stunned by what they encountered. A British officer describes entering Bergen-Belsen on April 15, 1945 in these words:

> As we walked down the main roadway of the camp, we were cheered by the internees, and for the first time we saw their condition. A great number were little more than living skeletons. There were men and women lying in heaps on both sides of the track. Others were walking slowly and aimlessly about, vacant expressions on their starved faces.

Those heaps contained thousands of bodies. The very fact that the bodies existed, however, suggests that Bergen-Belsen was not an extermination camp per se—in other words, that as infernal as it was, it was but a dot on the map compared to the killing center of Auschwitz. Unlike those gassed at Auschwitz, the starved of Bergen-Belsen suffered a "natural death." After liberation, some 17,000 inmates of Bergen-Belsen died of such "natural causes" as dysentery and typhus.

How then can so many have perished at Auschwitz—12,000 a day at one point—without the world noticing?

It is not that nothing was known of the mass slaughter while it was in progress. The story that the world was innocent of the truth until the facts suddenly broke upon it in 1945, more or less in the way the atomic bomb suddenly made its appearance before a shocked world that very year—this story is altogether unfounded. For those with eyes to see and ears to hear, the Holocaust was a fact all along. As Walter Laqueur has documented, there was an abundance of timely information of indisputable authenticity about the Holocaust. The point of his book The Terrible Secret is that the Holocaust was in fact an open secret, which is to say not really a secret at all. The Holocaust was about as secret as the secret police.

Nor was good information limited to government channels. Readers of The New York Times of July 2, 1942, for one example, were informed of "the slaughter of 700,000 Jews" in German-occupied Poland. Word of this massacre reached London through underground channels said to be absolutely reliable, even if the events themselves (as the Times observed) seemed too terrible and the atrocities too inhuman to be true. The report from Poland also notes that in the summer of 1941, Polish males between 14 and 60 "were herded into public squares and cemeteries, forced to dig their own graves and then were

machine-gunned and hand-grenaded"—Nazi trademarks. The Times article has a sub-head reading, "Gas Chambers Are Used."

For those close to the scenes of killing there was more forensic
evidence: the stench of the crematoria, the hair that went up the chimneys.

Treblinka was simply an open secret. As the commandant of the camp later recalled, "Hundreds of soldiers and civilians used to come up to our gate, stand along the fences, gawk, and try to buy things off us because it was known that there was all this stuff around." The stuff was plunder from the dead.

Among the documents compiled for the Nurem-berg trials after the war is a signed statement by an SS doctor dated May 16, 1942. It reads in part:

I ordered the vans of group D to be camouflaged as house-trailers by putting one set of window shutters on each side of the small van and two on each side of the larger vans, such as one often sees on farm houses in the country. The vans became so well-known, that not only the authorities but also the civilian population called the van 'death van,' as soon as one of these vehicles appeared. It is my opinion the van cannot be kept secret for any length of time, not even camouflaged.

But if a few death vans could not be kept secret, how could Treblinka, how could Auschwitz? The Holocaust was like tens of thousands of death vans, most imperfectly concealed.

A Penitent.

Reflecting on his own complicity, Hitler's architect and armaments minister Albert Speer wrote in 1970: "Whether I knew or did not know [of the Holocaust], or how much or how little I knew, is totally unimportant when I consider what horrors I ought to have known about and what conclusions would have been the natural ones to draw from the little I did know. No apologies are possible."

So the truth was not unknown so much as unregarded. There were a number of reasons for this, the most potent being that the facts themselves seemed beyond belief. That an entire people should be put to death, that their bodies should be incinerated by the million—this seemed outside the realm of possibility. Significantly, The New York Times story just quoted was put on page six, not because the editors thought the slaughter of 700,000 too minor a matter for the front page but rather (presumably) because they didn't know whether or not to believe such a staggering report at all. The generally dazed response to the Holocaust must have gratified Hitler, who claimed in Mein Kampf that a bold lie is more readily believed (since "the magnitude of the lie always contains a certain factor of credibility") and now saw his crimes disbelieved on account of their magnitude.

In the middle of the war, a Polish emissary, Jan Karski, met with Supreme Court Justice Felix Frankfurter to inform him of the ongoing murder of the Jewish people. "Frankfurter told Karski that he did not believe him. When Karski protested, Frankfurter explained that he did not imply that Karski had in any way not told the truth, he simply meant that he could not believe him—there was a difference"—Walter Laqueur, The Terrible Secret.

The principal reason, then, that news of the Holocaust was received with disbelief is that it seemed too monstrous to be true, even if the ruthlessness of the Nazis and the savagery of their propaganda were not in dispute.

It appears that many who knew it to be true still couldn't get themselves to believe it to be true. That contradiction seems to account for Felix Frankfurter's confused response to the news from Poland -- roughly,

"I accept it but I can't believe it"

-- and for the Times's confused handling of the same story. Without doubt many others, staggered by the sheer scale of the crime, responded with the same kind of shuddering disbelief. To admit the Holocaust was to admit that the world in which such a thing was not possible, not even conceivable, was gone.

Beginning on April 19, 1943, Jews of the Warsaw ghetto, using urban guerrilla tactics, took up arms against the Nazis. An SS general reported, "After a few days it was already clear that the Jews . . . were determined to fight back by every means and with the weapons in their possession." With a heavy advantage in numbers and armaments, the Germans vanquished Warsaw, but only after weeks. The guerrillas had to be sought out one by one.

One of the last messages sent from the Warsaw ghetto: "The world is silent; the world knows (it is inconceivable that it should not) and stays silent; God's vicar in the Vatican is silent; there is silence in London and Washington; the American Jews are silent. This silence is incomprehensible and horrifying."

In addition to the audacity of the event itself, other factors made the Holocaust hard for most to believe. Remembering the atrocity stories of World War I that proved false (such as tales of the Germans' use of corpses to make soap), people didn't want to be fooled "for the second time within one generation." The members of this school—those who closed their minds to the Holocaust, having decided to disbelieve any more reports of horror—provide an example of how not to think.

Also adding to the incredibility of the Holocaust was the sheer bombast of Hitler's rhetoric. If he proclaimed his intention to wipe out European Jewry (notably in his speech of January 30, 1939), he also proclaimed that the Third Reich would last a thousand years. Those inclined to disbelieve the Holocaust for one reason or another could tell themselves that Hitler's death sentence on the Jews was merely a rhetorical flourish like his operatic gestures—ignoring the grave assaults on the legal and human status of the Jews that had already taken place.

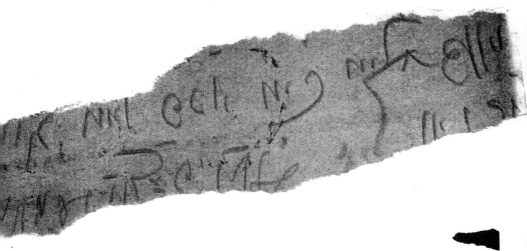

Many a Jew as well found it difficult to credit the Holocaust at the time. Under the influence both of historical experience and the human fear of the abyss, many saw or wished to see the "disappearance" of their fellows as one more persecution in the long line of persecutions of the

Jews rather than as what it was—an apocalyptic event wholly different in degree and kind from any historical precedent. The destruction of property; the massacre of innocents; even mass expulsion—all had befallen the Jews before, and not once but many times, so that the Jews who trembled to

acknowledge the terrible novelty of the Holocaust assimilated it to examples from the past. But nothing in the pages of the past, no slaughter, no expulsion, approached the scale of the Holocaust. People ask why the Jews did not resist their own execution (with the whispered implication that if they were abject enough to go to their death, they deserved it). The answer is that...

... some fought—as in the Warsaw ghetto or the uprisings at both Treblinka and Sobibor or the sabotage of Crematorium No. 3 in Auschwitz in October 1944—some hid, all knew that open resistance meant death, and many gave in to the all-too-human inclination to close their eyes to reality.

But of course it was not only the Jews who closed their eyes. So did great numbers of those with little or nothing at stake, and therefore with far less excuse. Further darkening this story is yet another reason the Holocaust was played down in the U. S. and Britain: government officials and perhaps editors as well feared that giving full public credence to the Holocaust would kindle the latent and not-so-latent anti-semitic feeling in their own countries. The notion that anti-semitism was confined to Germany— that the United States, for example, was quite free of it—is simply grotesque, as anyone acquainted with the hate-rhetoric of the thirties and the exclusionary practices of clubs, schools, and even entire towns in America can affirm. In a report on British public opinion, the Ministry of Information noted a flare-up of anti-semitism in Britain toward the end of 1942, coinciding with disclosures of the slaughter in the death camps.

Anti-semitism actually rose with the news—a violently irrational response, but one that rings true to the nature of bigotry. As analysts for the Ministry of Information concluded, information about the mass murder of European Jewry made the English "more conscious of the Jews they do not like here."

And so for reasons of prudence, public acknowledgment of the Holocaust was muted. In 1941, indeed, a committee of the Ministry of Information had advised that propaganda for domestic consumption go lightly on Hitler's atrocities and focus only on "indisputably innocent people. Not Jews."

Nor was the United States any more enlightened. Here too, in all likelihood, there were those who feared that giving full public credence to the Holocaust would be taken as a play for sympathy for the Jews or as confirmation of Jewish influence, or would divert the country from the more urgent goal of defeating the military machines of Japan and Germany.

On May 13, 1939, the *SS St. Louis* sailed from Germany bound for Havana, Cuba with 936 passengers, 930 of whom were Jewish refugees from the Nazis. For 734 refugees, Cuba was just a way station en route to the safety of the United States.

None of the passengers were aware, however, that eight days earlier, the Cuban president had signed a decree invalidating their landing certificates. As this news spread among the ship, many passengers felt that if Cuba forced the ship to return to Germany, surely the United States would intervene to save their lives. But the US offered no compromise in its immi-

gration laws, knowing full well the probable fate for the *St. Louis'* passengers. The ship returned to Europe where passengers eventually were sent to Belgium, England, Holland and France.

However, on September 1, 1939, World War II began with the German invasion of Poland. The only *SS St. Louis* refugees spared the fatal wrath of the Nazis were those who found sanctuary in Britain. Many of the others died in German gas chambers following the Nazi invasions of Belgium, Holland and France.

But are we to believe that Washington and London played down the Holocaust solely to avoid inflaming the anti-semitism of the domestic population? Surely a less handsome motive was at work—something other than rational prudence and a decent concern for the welfare of Jews.

Washington and London were cool to the fate of the Jews because they were Jews. The civilized men of these capitals did not go in for the rabid anti-semitism of Hitler, but that doesn't mean they were untouched by anti-semitism altogether.

(That anti-semitism and "civilization" go together well enough is shown by the example of T. S. Eliot, if proof were needed.) The men of Washington and London had other things on their minds besides the annihilation of the Jews. They were not fighting on behalf of the Jews, any more than the North went to war on behalf of the slaves in the Civil War.

Writes Gitta Sereny, "For a variety of political and emotional reasons, the American government—perhaps even more than the British—was wary of seeming to fight 'a war for the Jews'." Who can doubt what those political and emotional reasons were?

The story is told that after his escape from the Warsaw ghetto a famous rabbi was invited to see Winston Churchill and advise him on how to bring about Germany's defeat. The rabbi (the story goes) replied as follows: "There are two possible ways, one involving natural means, the other supernatural. The natural means would be if a million angels with flaming swords were to descend on Germany and destroy it. The supernatural would be if a million Englishmen parachuted down on Germany and destroyed it." Churchill, being a realist, chose the natural method, angels with flaming swords.

Following the war, researchers on American anti-semitism found people expressing sentiments like this:

"I don't blame the Nazis at all for what they did to the Jews. That sounds terrible, I know, but if the Jews acted the way they do here, I don't blame them...

I've never had any bad personal experiences with Jews, it's just the way they act. Don't help your fellow man: that's their creed." To someone with this mentality it is only fitting that there was no help for the Jews when they were sent to their death.

It would be nice to think that anti-semitism simply burned itself out in the great conflagration of the Holocaust. It did not. Like the phoenix it rises from its own ruins.

For the Nazis, killing the Jews was not enough—they must add touches of refinement like making Jews clean out the ovens and then using the ashes to pave the garden walks of the SS. Those who were still complaining about the Jews in 1946—for them too, it seems, mere slaughter was not enough.

Rabid anti-semitism: "Even though the rage of the people sometimes flares high against the eternal blood-sucker, it does not in the least prevent him from reappearing in a few years in the place he had hardly left and beginning the old life all over again. No persecution can deter him from his type of human exploitation."—Hitler, "Mein Kampf."

Tepid anti-semitism: "Well, no one could call me anti-semitic, but I do think the way these Jews behave is too absolutely stinking. The way they push their way to the head of queues, and so on. They're so abominably selfish. I think they're responsible for a lot of what happens to them"—a middle-class Englishwoman quoted by George Orwell in 1945.

Never before had the Jews been subjected to the Nazis' kind of "coordination," a word that took on murderous meaning. The coordinator of the Holocaust was Adolf Eichmann, the official of the Reich Security Headquarters in charge of "Jewish Affairs." It was Eichmann who saw to the deportation of the Jews of Europe nation by nation. Though he fired no weapon and released no gas, though he operated far from killing centers like Auschwitz, Eichmann came to be considered by many the executioner of the Jewish people since he "selected" the victims in the first place and arranged the logistics of death. By his own admission he was "at the center of everything connected with Jewish affairs." Eichmann was the dispatcher of the "Final Solution."

When over 400,000 Hungarian Jews were shipped to Auschwitz in but two months, it was he who requisitioned the trains. When the heroic Raoul Wallenberg went to Budapest in June 1944 to provide Jews with Swedish passports, it was Eichmann he was saving them from. After the war Primo Levi would address a poem of rage to Eichmann.

It was also Eichmann who convened the Wannsee Conference where the "Final Solution" was put into motion. The man acted the role of the facilitator, as it is called today. He facilitated the death of the Jews of Europe. (After the war it seems Eichmann learned to prattle like a facilita-

tor, too. He had worked for "solutions" that would "benefit all concerned," he had shared the Jews' interests, etc.) Eichmann was also, though he later denied it, in on the decision to use Zyklon-B at Auschwitz, and like the authorities at Auschwitz came to exercise a power above and beyond legality itself—a power, that is,  authorized by Hitler's will and not by ordinary human statutes. In Nazi jargon, Eichmann's powers were "special," as the treatment accorded the Jews was also "special."

In May of 1960 Eichmann was seized by Israeli agents in Argentina, flown back to Israel and tried for causing the death of millions and for crimes against humanity.

Reporting on this historic trial for the New Yorker, Hannah Arendt was struck by the unlikeliness of the man who had sent millions to their death.

Though his crimes staggered the imagination, he himself seemed undemonic, more like an ordinary bureaucrat than anything else, a man without mania or genius -- "banality" incarnate.

At one point his own attorney likened him to "a common mailman," and one can envision Eichmann sorting Jews onto trains like so many parcels. (He called them shipments.) In the world of normalized murder Adolf Eichmann was a normal man.

The sheer improbability of this war criminal came out in his pre-trial interrogation by a member of the Israeli police whose father had been deported to his death by Eichmann. Through the hours of questioning Eichmann represents himself as a softie, a man whose knees went weak at Auschwitz, who had nothing to do with Zyklon-B and nothing to do with killing, who had the interests of the Jews at heart, who wrote the invitations to the Wannsee Conference and during it sat unregarded in the corner with a stenographer, like a sort of wallflower of genocide. Even allowing for a good deal of whitewash in his account of himself, Eichmann simply does not answer our mental image of a mass murderer or the traditional image of evil as twisted genius. The engineer of the "Final Solution" seemed more like a desk clerk than a mastermind.

From Eichmann's statement: "We drove to a certain place—I don't know my way around Auschwitz. I never got further than the command post at the main entrance. Had no desire to. As we were driving, I saw some big buildings. Almost like factories. Enormous chimneys. Höss [Commandant of Auschwitz] says to me: 'Working to capacity! Ten thousand!' A job was under way. They were separating the able-bodied from the ones who were supposedly unfit for work. I didn't watch the gassing. I couldn't. I'd have probably keeled over. And I thought: Whew, I've got it over with. But then he drives me to a big trench. . . And there was an enormous grating, an iron grating. And corpses were burning on it. Then I got sick to my stomach. Sick to my stomach."

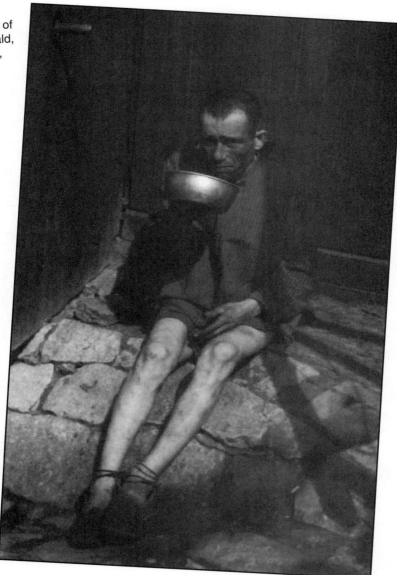

A survivor of
Buchenwald,
October 3,
1945.

As Hannah Arendt observed Eichmann in Jerusalem, she came to believe that it was the thoughtlessness of the man—not negligence or stupidity, but plain lack of thought—that enabled him to do what he did. To Hannah Arendt Eichmann was a mental blank. Years later, still haunted by the weirdness of the man, she wrote that instead of thought his mind knew only clichés. He had after all even gone to the gallows uttering clichés.

The Last Words of Adolf Eichmann

"After a short while, gentlemen, we shall all meet again. [He had just declared he was no Christian.] Such is the fate of all men. Long live Germany, long live Argentina, long live Austria. I shall not forget them."

Although Hannah Arendt's account of Eichmann was disputed, there is much on the record to support her reading. The man even talked about being unthinking. In his desk-work, he told his interrogator, "you didn't waste your time thinking about unconditional allegiances, unconditional loyalty, because you threw yourself head over heels into your—into your—work." Ideology is not all Eichmann didn't waste time thinking about. He put people on trains and never thought of what awaited them at the other end, even after he had seen with his own eyes. In Jerusalem he maintained over and over that he had "nothing to do with the killing. With the evacuation, yes—I can't wriggle out of that, I have to admit it. But once a shipment [sic] was delivered to the designated station as per the decisions of the scheduling conference, my powers ceased." And this was Eichmann's story—he deported Jews to the

camps (always under orders), and without question millions were put to death there, but his own responsibility ended at the camp gate. Almost as if a person were to say, Yes I fired the gun, and of course Smith fell dead, but after all the bullet killed him, I didn't.

What could Eichmann have been thinking when he took this line? Did he really think anyone mentally awake would buy his excuses? If Eichmann can plead his own blindness, why can't the camp commandant plead his own hardness of heart? Most likely Hannah Arendt is right and Eichmann didn't think at all. When he complained that "propaganda transformed me into a person I never was," it did not occur to the man that Nazi propaganda did just that to the Jews. No cognizant person could have talked the way Eichmann did.

No cognizant person could have claimed, as he did over and over, that shipping Jews to Auschwitz was "pure transportation. It has nothing to do with killing." No cognizant person could have imagined that the children of those he sent to death would accept his tender of friendship. Yet Eichmann declared in Jerusalem that he wanted to "find peace with my former enemies," the Jews, the same Jews he had, in his own words, "delivered to the butcher." Maybe he imagined a tearful embrace, and all forgiven. Maybe it was a belief

Nazis rounding up Jews in Krakow, Poland, 1941

that he had no more choice than the Jews he deported (being bound by orders) that led him to imagine a bond between them. But the argument that he was just as hapless as those he shipped to their death—the argument that he, Adolf Eichmann, was just as much a victim as they—is itself a crime against humanity.

"I had no luck," Eichmann said in Jerusalem.

If Eichmann possessed no great abilities, not even (though this is uncertain) any exceptional ideological drive, how was he able to commit such crimes? How could this nullity, this void "at the center of everything," be responsible for so much?

Several factors had to be in place for Adolf Eichmann to rise to the level of a war criminal.

• The work of dispatching Jews to their death had to be routine, as mechanical a process as running the trains or indeed handling the mail. In other words, it had to be bureaucratized. (If Eichmann was a nobody, Hannah Arendt once defined bureaucracy as rule by nobody.)

• A language not only permitting but positively commanding mass murder had to be in place in order to give killing the appearance of a duty. With its portrayal of the Jews as a pestilence, Nazi discourse performed this function.

• At the same time, there had to be layers of insulation between Eichmann and the killing itself. If the man is to be believed, he could not endure the sight of murder. (Others peered into the gas chambers like a peep show.) It was the division of labor that allowed Eichmann to leave the execution of the Jews to others while concentrating on his own "duty." With the division of labor, in turn, goes the hardening of routines: and so the circle closes.

One doesn't have to be miles away from the scene of killing to achieve a sense of removal. When the commandant of Sobibor (later the commandant of Treblinka) was asked after the war how he felt about the mass murders in his own camp, he answered,

"At Sobibor one could avoid seeing almost all of it—it all happened so far away from the camp-buildings."

Jewish women and their children before their execution by the Einsatzgruppen, Mizocz Poland, 1942

The twentieth century has refined the technology for killing at a distance. The Nazi system enabled killers at the very scene of murder to do their work with a sense of being far away.

Curiously, Franz Stangl portrays himself just as Eichmann did in Jerusalem: as a man of good will, a hapless victim of Nazism, a tender-hearted sufferer who was appalled at the sight of pits filled with corpses, an innocent who had nothing to do with the mass killings that went on under his own authority and whose role in events was purely "administrative." Was it sheer desperation that led both of these arch-criminals to the same strategies of evasion?

Victims of Circumstance?

Is it really true that Eichmann and Stangl and all the others who disclaimed their own actions were simply victims of circumstance, helplessly caught up in events over which they had no control?

"As the expert witnesses in the Auschwitz trials [in then-West Germany] demonstrated in great detail a quarter century ago, no one became an executioner in an extermination camp without having taken moral decisions at a number of possible escape points along the way. Not only was it possible to avoid joining the SS, or, once in, to avoid being posted to an extermination camp, or, once there, to avoid having to commit acts of murder and brutality, it was also possible to extricate oneself from these situations or even use them to try and help the victims. Difficult though such choices were, a small number of Germans did indeed take them, and not always at the cost of their own lives"—Richard J. Evans, "In Hitler's Shadow: West German Historians and the Attempt to Escape from the Nazi Past" (1989).

A class of Jewish children, all wearing the Jewish star in accordance with Nazi regulations. In the second row, second from right, squinting, is Yoka Verdoner, who survived the war in hiding. The fate of the other children is not known. Netherlands, 1942.

Consider the children sent to the gas chamber, like the children of Fossoli: those are victims of circumstance. For their own executioners to take the word "victims" for themselves is just as appalling as it was for the Nazis to make Jews operate the crematoria or indeed to project their own plans for world domination onto the Jews in the first place. In a way, it enacts the Holocaust all over again.

Zyklon-B made it possible to kill with an efficiency never known before, but it was the language of Nazism that both sanctified and mystified the killing process. Nazi language was the signed death-warrant for the Jews of Europe that has never been found. Especially murderous was the system of bureaucratic code-words the Nazis used alongside the public jabber of "the folk" and "blood and soil." It was on the rails of code-words that Nazism ran.

Here then are some of the code-words of Nazism—along with their real meanings:

A "DICTIONARY" OF NAZI CODE-WORDS

• **"The Final Solution of the Jewish Problem"**—code for the extinction of European Jewry. "Final" in the sense that no Jew should remain alive. "Solution" meaning an answer to a purely technical question, such as how to dispose of waste. "Jewish problem" meaning the Jews are the problem. In the words of author Raul Hilberg, the phrase "final solution of the Jewish problem" suggests "crossing a psychological threshold, scoring an administrative breakthrough, making no exceptions, and halting before no consequences."

• **"Evacuation"**—deportation to slavery and death. A reversal of normal usage, where the term means being removed from danger to a place of safety.

• **"Special treatment"**—death, usually by gassing. Eichmann was asked about the meaning of this favored euphemism. "Q: What does 'special treatment' mean, and who was subjected to it? A: Special treatment was killing. Who thought up the term—I don't know. Q: But you knew special treatment meant killing? A: Everybody knew that, yes, Herr Hauptmann, everybody knew. When a shipment was marked 'for special treatment,' they decided at the point of arrival who was fit for labor and who wasn't."

• **"Shipment"**—Jews sent to death, roughly a thousand per train.

Nuremberg Document NO-2363

SS-Lieutenant Colonel Liebehenschel to
Concentration Camp Auschwitz

August 26, 1942

Permission is hereby given for dispatch of a truck to Dessau to load material for special treatment. Permit is to be given to the driver.

• **"Labor service"**—slavery or gassing; that is, eventual or immediate death. The fiction that Auschwitz was purely a labor camp is enshrined in the sign still standing over the gate: "Arbeit macht frei"— Work makes you free. A more fitting motto would be the one at the entrance to Dante's Hell: "Abandon all hope ye who enter here."

• **"Bath," "shower"**—gas chamber.

• **"Special action," "action"**—mass murder. Particularly but not exclusively used for the deeds of the Einsatzgruppen. (In the 1930s, before the stage of mass murder, the term "action" was used for group arrests by the Gestapo.)

• **"Einsatzgruppen"** ("Prompt-Employment Units")—killing squads.

• **"Natural reduction"**—death in ghettoes or camps by starvation or disease.

• **"Euthanasia," "mercy death"**—the killing of undesirables, sometimes singly, under the cover of medical procedure.

• **"Protective custody"**—imprisonment in a concentration camp.

• **"Language-rules"**—the system of verbal camouflage made up of terms such as those glossed here. Like something too holy to be spoken of by name, everything connected with the annihilation of the Jews of Europe, even the system of verbal cover itself, had its cover-word.

And so if the Nazis openly gloried in sadism, butchered hundreds of thousands in the open air of the U.S.S.R., caricatured the Jews with all possible grossness—if in so many ways the Nazis shouted their intentions to the world, they also concealed their actions under a fog of euphemisms and kept the Holocaust semi-secret enough that the world was able to pretend it was not happening.

Maybe it was the sense of being well concealed by some kind of camouflage (as Eichmann claimed to be "covered" in whatever he did) that inspired the Nazis to go so far in carrying out their vision of the purification of Europe. Or they may have believed that the very scale of their crime would make it

undetectable, for by incinerating every last Jew they would at the same time be destroying the evidence. An SS man taunted his prisoners: "We will destroy the evidence together with you."

The other side of the spectacle and fanfare of Nazi "culture," then, was the quiet routines of death. In contrast to the bombast of Nazi rhetoric, the grand conclusion of the Nazi race policy—the gas chamber—was a kind of state secret, spoken of in whispers and double-meanings. This made it holy and kept it from being questioned, as the SS in Auschwitz kept from asking forbidden questions.

The air of unspeakable mystery must have stirred the hearts of the Nazis as they crossed the last threshold and were initiated into the brotherhood of murder.

For the Nazis, carrying out the ideology meant making it come true—by force. So it is that when the Allies entered Bergen-Belsen they found a camp ravaged by typhus. Having portrayed the Jews as a deadly disease, the Nazis made them carriers of disease. (Recall that elsewhere prisoners had actually been injected with typhus.) Having ridiculed the haunted faces of expressionism as "degenerate art," the Nazis etched those faces onto the Jewish prisoners they called degenerates, and when the liberators of the camps finally came they were met by faces so hollow and ghostly, so sunken and possessed that such visions had only been seen before on an artist's canvas, if there.

The same drive for the absolute that made the Nazis detest the half-measures and delays of parliamentary democracy led them to attempt to "solve" the Jewish question for all time. And along with the will to realize their vision in ultimate terms went a need to clothe their actions in an elaborate show of bureaucratic propriety—the stenographer at the Wannsee Conference; the stacks of documents; Eichmann and his orders from above. It is one of the contradictions of Mein Kampf that Hitler views the Germans as a higher race even as he holds the German masses in contempt, fit only to be deceived by one like himself. But the Nazis may have used deception on

themselves as well as others. Their code of secrecy, their use of double-entendres, their tip-toeing around forbidden topics, their charade of obedience to supreme Law, their fiction of a clean murder that leave no evidence—all these mental devices emboldened them to carry out their ideology to the last degree of its murderous implications.

Could the Holocaust have been averted? Could the Nazis' campaign against the Jews have been halted at some point short of the "Final Solution"? The historian Conor Cruise O'Brien believes so.

The key, O'Brien thinks, lies with the German churches, which alone possessed the moral force and the collective voice to make Hitler back down. Writing in the New York Review of Books of April 27, 1989, O'Brien theorizes that if the churches had raised their voice against the persecution of the Jews, the Holocaust could well have been prevented. In particular the Catholic Church, with its doctrinal unity—its means to pro-

claim the same message from every pulpit—had the power to make itself heard, and in fact a 1937 pastoral letter from Pope Pius XI condemning "the idolatrous cult of Volk and Race" was read aloud in all Catholic church-

es in Germany, much to the anger of the Nazis. (It also referred to the Jews as the people who put Christ on the cross.) Soon after, a stronger pronouncement was drafted for the Pope, but unhappily it was never published, for upon his death in 1939 the papacy went to Pius XII, who was careful never to antagonize Hitler. When some 600 Jews were sent to their death from Fossoli in February 1944, it was Pius XII who made no objection.

Earlier, voices of objection had been heard. An immediate precursor of the Holocaust was the so-called euthanasia program, in which thousands of the ill and insane were "granted a mercy death." Perhaps because the victims included non-Jews, this atrocity was denounced by the German churches—denounced with such

force that the T4 program was officially suspended. It is this demonstration of the efficacy of religious protest that lends some weight to the theory that the Holocaust itself could possibly have been averted by a determined effort of the German churches. But no such effort was made. The fact is that the Protestant churches of Germany were in bed with National Socialism and preserved a discreet silence when such atrocities as the Kristallnacht took place under their very eyes.

The Voice of the Vatican

"On November 27, 1940, one year and two months after the official beginning of the Euthanasia Program [T4], the Holy Office met in conclave and made its first official statement on the subject of euthanasia. But even this, the mildest of pronouncements, stating that the 'extinction of unworthy life by public mandate [was] incompatible with natural and divine law,' was only mentioned once, in Latin, on the Vatican radio, and in the Osservatore Romano, equally in Latin, of course"—Gitta Sereny, Into That Darkness.

Smoke fills the sky during the Warsaw ghetto uprising, 1943.

As we know, the Nazis did not launch the Holocaust all at once but built up to it incrementally, testing their methods, their resolve, and their opposition. Opposition from the churches, they learned, was a potential danger but not, all in all, a grave one. It did not amount to that much.

In fact it did not even put an end to the "euthanasia." The program was simply hushed up, wrapped in the official silence, the controlled mystery, that was later to surround the work of mass extermination. The cessation of T4 did not halt the progress toward the "Final Solution." The killing only expanded. It would have taken more than isolated acts of bravery by a few pastors, more even than a sharply worded papal encyclical to avert the massacre of European Jewry. An encyclical might have helped as O'Brien claims, but in all likelihood would not have been enough to offset the massive complicity of the German people, the virulence of anti-semitic propaganda, and the sheer blind momentum that Nazism had already gathered by 1939.

In any case, if the Catholic Church had led the resistance to Hitler (a classic example of a contrary-to-fact supposition), it could only have been by taking "a fully publicized, unequivocal moral stand" (Gitta Sereny). Opposition to be effective had to be open and wholehearted. Probably the closest approximation to such a stand is to be found among the Danes.

The resistance to the Nazis offered by the Danes is a singular example of effective protest—effective because it was fully public, and popular as well as official.

As an act of solidarity with the Jews, the King of Denmark informed the Nazis that he himself would wear the yellow badge, and when the date of the deportation of the Jews from Denmark was set, "all sections of the Danish people, from the King down to simple citizens" stood ready to aid them, as the Eichmann tribunal later recorded. In consequence of this deep-rooted resistance, relatively few of the Danish Jews fell into Nazi hands. This, then, is the kind of opposition that would have been necessary within Germany to stop Nazism in its tracks. But of course it was Nazism itself that commanded popular loyalty there, and held the state.

When several thousand Jews with non-Jewish wives were collected in Berlin for deportation to Auschwitz, it is said that the women staged a public vigil and demanded the return of their men. Even in the face of the SS they held firm. And incredibly, it appears that their husbands were returned—returned from the very gates of death. (This story is told by Gerda Lerner, herself a refugee from Nazi Germany, in the Progressive of March 1994.) If open resistance like this had been the rule instead of a most exotic exception, the Jews of Europe might conceivably have been save

Public humiliation of Jews: one Jew is forced to cut the beard of another under German supervision while the local population watches. Tomaszow Mazowiecki, Poland, c. 1939.

SOME FALLACIES

- **"The Holocaust never happened. It is a Jewish invention."**

This, the neo-Nazi line (now illegal in Germany), takes up where Nazism left off. Where the original Nazis stripped the Jews of their rights, their property, their flesh, their lives, and finally even their graves, the neo-Nazis strip the Jews of their very deaths. This is just as the SS would have had it. But in a way, the neo-Nazis go the original Nazis one better, for they seem to be saying that the Jews deserve a second Holocaust for making up monstrous tales about a first one.

- **"Every time the innocent are slaughtered, it is a Holocaust."**

While at least acknowledging the murder of the Jews (more or less), this argument refuses to reckon with the sheer dimensions of the event and the incomparable nature of the Nazis' killing machine. Behind the claim that the Holocaust is just one mass murder among many is probably some vague liberal sentiment like "people are the same everywhere" as well as a resent-

Nazi students at the book burning unload the "un-German" books. The banner on the back of the truck reads: "German students march against the un-German spirit." Berlin, Germany, May 1933.

ment of the "privilege" accorded the murdered Jews among so many other victims. In other words, the argument is a banality with some admixture of spite. Ex-Nazis for their part have pointed to war crimes committed by the US in Vietnam (which were real enough) to argue that there was nothing particularly heinous or even special about what they themselved did; war is war, they say, and every war is a slaughter. Their response to the Holocaust, like that of many others, comes down to two words: "So what?"

• "Next to the Holocaust, the suffering of other peoples does not count."

The scope of the Holocaust, incomprehensibly vast as it is, does not diminish the significance of the carnage inflicted on other peoples, such as the Indian tribes of North America or the enslaved peoples of Africa. The idea of groups competing for top status in some hierarchy of victimhood is grotesque. Nor for that matter does the Holocaust confer moral authority on the Jews as a people.

• "Everyone has their own personal Holocaust."

Those who take this line seem to be saying, "Don't leave me out! I want to be considered a victim too!" As though attacking elitism, they cry out that they too deserve victim status. Everyone who lives through child abuse, they say, lives through Auschwitz. Their argument, a compound of puerility and mistaken envy, robs the Holocaust of all specificity by likening the execution of an entire people to an unhappy childhood. Additionally, the claim that everyone is a victim falls right in with the prevarications of men like Eichmann and Stangl, both of whom considered themselves just as out of luck as those they condemned to death. Incredible to report, this was the very line taken by then-President Reagan when he made his infamous visit to the military cemetery in Bitburg, Germany, where SS men as well as ordinary soldiers lie buried. Referring to the SS, Reagan declared, "Those young men are victims of Nazism also. . . . They were victims, just as surely as the victims in the concentration camps."

• "We are all responsible for the Holocaust."

Like the claim that everyone has a Holocaust, this statement seems motivated by some pained wish not to leave anyone out, some urge to extend a kind of "membership" in the Holocaust universally. Though heart-warming, it doesn't stand up to analysis.

As someone has said, where all are responsible, none are responsible. If all are responsible, then Eichmann was no more responsible for the Holocaust than anyone else, which is in effect what he claimed. Insipid pieties like "we are all responsible" serve admirably to cloud specific questions like who did what.

The burning of the synagogue in Ober Ramstadt during Kristallnacht. The local fire department prevented the fire from spreading to a nearby home, but made no attempt to intervene in the synagogue fire. Ober Ramstadt, Germany, November 9, 1938.

Probably there are many in France today who would sooner admit that "all are responsible" than see the archives opened. They know that line is a whitewash. And what of those who hid Jews from the Nazis, as some did in France—are they too responsible for the Holocaust because "all" are? Are they just as responsible as their neighbors who betrayed the Jews or looked the other way?

Women prisoners at work in the camp quarry at Plaszow, Poland, 1944.

- **"The Jews did not die in vain, because now we know how to prevent a second Holocaust."**

  One Holocaust is enough.

- **"I still believe that people are good at heart."**

With both the Red and Allied armies approaching and their cause lost, the SS did not call an end to the torture and murder of their captives. No: they marched them toward the center of Germany, evidently to prevent their liberation and to keep them from bearing witness to the murder of European Jewry. As far as the SS was concered, if thousands perished on these forced marches, so much the better.

This was the season of the Nazis' farewell.

Slave laborers on the day of their liberation from the Buchenwald camp. Elie Wiesel appears as the last full face on the second bunk from the bottom (in the circle on the facing page). Buchenwald, Germany, April 16, 1945.

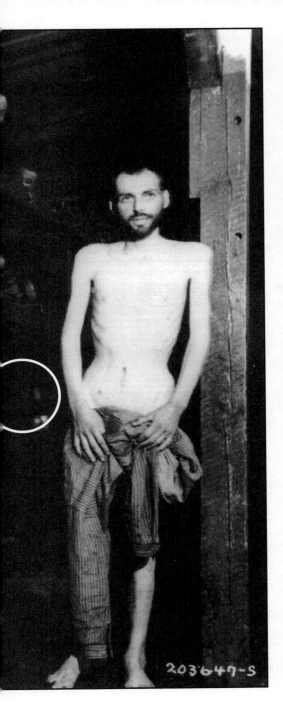

To kill while the killing was good, camp authorities in Leipzig locked 300 forced laborers in a hut and set it afire. As a parting shot the SS in Gardelegen suffocated 1800 in the same manner, then poured kerosene on the dead and set them ablaze. The Allies came upon the corpses. The good citizens of Gardelegen were ordered to bury the charred remains in individual graves, each body in its own coffin.

When Generals Patton, Bradley and Eisenhower entered the slave-labor camp of Ohrdruf on April 4, 1945, they discovered such scenes of horror that Patton became ill and Eisenhower ordered all units in the vicinity to the scene to survey the camp with their own eyes.

In Dora, near Nordhausen, 80 were hanged in February 1945 for building a radio transmitter. Seventy-five more were hanged on March 10, 12 more on March 13. When the Americans entered Nordhausen they found hundreds of unburied corpses of the victims of hunger, along with living prisoners so debilitated by starvation that they lay in the same bed with a corpse, so racked with thirst that they drank urine. As is reported in the documents assembled for the Nuremberg Trials, "Some effort had been made to burn some of the bodies, and the partially burned, blackened bodies of 100 children lay about the premises"—giving new meaning to the policy of "scorched earth."

In April when British troops entered Bergen-Belsen, they came upon a scene beyond human imagination.

The surviving inmates of the camp lived and moved among piles of corpses—the

hideously emaciated frames of thousands who had succumbed to hunger and disease, corpses in heaps like the stacks of crutches left behind in a great cathedral by the healed. British cameras filmed the event. The resulting footage contains perhaps the most ghastly scenes ever recorded. As if in testimoy to the unspeakable nature of the Nazis' crimes, much of the film proceeds in silence.

The Nazis, as we know, not only murdered but taunted their victims,

and so it is that before the liberation of Bergen-Belsen, they had forced those still alive to drag the bodies of the dead one by one to a monstrous dump, as though reminding them of the end awaiting them. It was fitting, therefore, that the British in turn com-

pelled the SS (whom they found well-fed, cheerful, and totally unrepentant) to drag the thousands of corpses still remaining to great burial pits. The corpses themselves are figures of horror—not just naked but fleshless, and on many of the faces a terrible image of the famous Scream painted by Edvard Munch.

One by one the bodies are hauled by the SS to the pits—some fifteen thousand in all. The burghers of the town are made to watch the proceedings, many of them no doubt outraged at the British. Then the bulldozers are called in and the pits filled with earth.

As you watch the SS men carting corpses and flinging them into the pit—breaking the bones of the dead in one last gesture of barbarism—a voice rises up in you: "Bury them! When the last of those stick-corpses goes into the pit, the SS go in too. Don't allow them to slip back into normal civilian life like an assassin melting into the crowd—don't put them on trial and give them a chance to portray themselves as victims of hard luck. No: give them the fate that befits them. Bury them alive. Let them dwell with their own victims. Let them learn what it is to die accursed."

And yet they were permitted to live.

Where did the British find their restraint? What kept them from plowing the Germans into the pit where they belonged? Maybe they had seen enough barbarity and thought it behoved them to act like civilized human beings.

At Auschwitz, an orchestra made up of inmates performed at the departure and return of work battalions. This photograph was taken from a window in Block 24 and was used as evidence in the trial of Rudolf Höss. Auschwitz, Poland, summer 1941.

The above illustration shows the locations of eight German concentration camps. **The illustration below** gives the approximate Jewish populations of European countries at 1941, followed by the number of Jews exterminated by 1945.

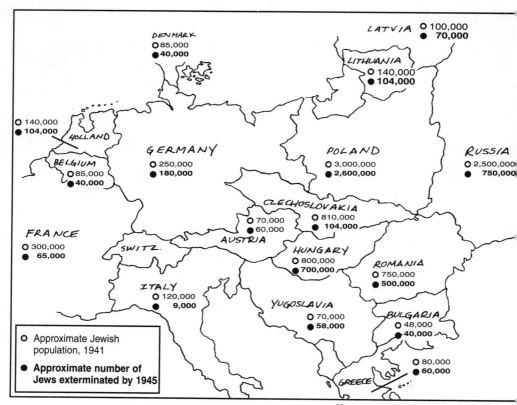

○ Approximate Jewish population, 1941

● **Approximate number of Jews exterminated by 1945**

Maps created by Quincy Justman
Source: Richard J. Evans, "*In Hitler's Sha*

Timelines

January 1939:	Hitler announces his intention to exterminate European Jewry.
June 1941:	Germany invades Soviet Union: Einsatzgruppen go into action.
December 1941:	Chelmno concentration camp opened in Poland.
January 1942:	Wannsee Conference; "Final Solution" plotted.
March 1942:	Mass transports arrive at Auschwitz.
July 1942:	Killing begins at Treblinka. Deportations from occupied Europe.
January 1943:	Some 2.5 to 3 million Jews killed to date.
Summer 1944:	Eichmann's "shipments" from Hungary to Auschwitz.
By war's end:	Between 1 and 2 million Jews killed in Auschwitz alone. Total number of Jews killed: approximately 6 million.

Sources

Arendt, Hannah. *Eichmann in Jerusalem*. The controversial account of Eichmann's trial.

Bettelheim, Bruno. *Surviving*. Essays by the noted psychoanalyst, himself a survivor of Dachau and Buchenwald.

Eichmann Interrogated. Transcripts from the Archives of the Israeli Police. Primary source.

Eliach, Yaffa. *Hasidic Tales of the Holocaust*.

Elton, G. R. Essay on the history of anti-semitism in *The New York Review of Books*, Jan. 19, 1989.

Evans, Richard J. *In Hitler's Shadow: West German Historians and the Attempt to Escape from the Nazi Past*. Critical study of recent German apologists for Nazism.

Hilberg, Raul. *Documents of Destruction*. Primary sources.

Hitler, Adolf. *Mein Kampf*.

Laqueur, Walter. *The Terrible Secret*. Explodes the myth that the Holocaust was a secret.

Levi, Primo. *Survival in Auschwitz and The Drowned and the Saved*. Memories and meditations by a survivor of Auschwitz.

Lifton, Robert J. *Nazi Doctors*. Contains interviews with doctors who presided over genocide.

Morse, Arthur D. *While Six Million Died.*

Nazi Conspiracy and Aggression. Multi-volume collection of documents assembled for the Nuremberg tribunal.

O'Brien, Conor Cruise. "A Lost Chance to Save the Jews?" *The New York Review of Books*, April 27, 1989.

Pfaff, William. Barbarian Sentiments. Historical reflections.

Sereny, Gitta. Into That Darkness. In-depth interview with Franz Stangl, commandant of Treblinka.

Steiner, George. Language and Silence. Contains thoughts on the deformation of language by Nazism.

Photographs

The publishers would like to express their gratitude to the United States Holocaust Memorial Museum, 100 Raoul Wallenberg Place, SW, Washington, DC, and Ms. Vivian Boxer in particular, for their help in making available all of the photographs printed in this book. All photos are courtesy of the museum and credited to the following:

Page 5: National Archives, Washington, DC.

Page 7: Main Commission for the Investigation of Nazi War Crimes, Warsaw.

Page 9: Jewish Historical Institute, Warsaw.

Page 16: National Archives, Suitland, MD.

Page 20: National Archives, Washington, DC.

Page 23: National Archives, Washington, DC.

Page 42: Jewish Cultural Society, Kiev, Ukraine.

Page 44: National Archives, Washington, DC.

Page 47: Estelle Bechhoefer.

Page 52: National Archives, Washington, DC.

Pages 70-71: National Archives, Washington, DC.

Page 73: National Archives, Washington, DC.

Page 81: National Archives, Washington, DC.

Page 84: State Archive of Krakow, Krakow, Poland.

Page 87: Main Commission for the Investigation of nazi War Crimes, Warsaw.

Page 88: Fran Verdoner Kan.

Page 90: Estelle Bechhoefer.

Page 94: Jewish Historical Institute, Warsaw; State Archive of Krakow, Krakow, Poland.

Page 95: *both photos,* National Archives, Washington, DC.

Photographs

Index

Index

DATE DUE

NOV 1 5 1999			
5-9-01	131,0902		
AR 31 04			
GAYLORD			PRINTED IN U.S.A